Photo Courtesy of Mary Vail, OSG, Publicist

DEDICATION

TO OUR FAMILIES,

Without your patience and love this book would not have been possible.

Thank you, Mark, Alana, Joe Jr., David, Sean, and Ashley, for encouraging our wild endeavors and allowing us the freedom to pursue our innovative spirits.

ACKNOWLEDGMENTS

We acknowledge those who supported our endeavor to recognize and celebrate the work of the visionaries, innovators, and artisans honored in this book. Unsurprisingly, the support came from individuals and organizations who personify all of these diverse talents in the industry.

It requires a team to achieve winning projects, and the GAVA team was instrumental in the success of this inaugural competition.

Structure Studios: Noah Nehlich, Joe Macchiaverna, Stephanie Dunn, JR Rapp, Ross Horvitz, and Farid Mokraoui.

Zodiac Pool Systems/Jandy: Vance Gillette, David Nibler, Bob Haning, and Tessa Boulware.

Paramount Pool & Spa Systems: Buzz Ghiz, Bill Burt, and Molly Hammant.

BRAND, Ltd: Pam Cirulli, Carin Kwon, Jessica Pfeifle, and Becky Bosshart.

The Art Institute of Las Vegas: Steven E. Brooks and Anne Dean.

Schiffer Publishing: Nancy Schiffer and Tina Skinner.

Photo Courtesy of Mary Vail, OSG, Publicist

INTERNATIONAL AWARD-WINNING
POOLS, SPAS, & WATER ENVIRONMENTS

Virginia Martino, Joseph M. Vassallo, and Mary Vail

Schiffer Publishing Ltd®
4880 Lower Valley Road, Atglen, PA 19310

Presented by GAVA

Disclaimer

Information and images submitted for a GAVA were provided by the entrant. Entrants certified that all information, data, and images submitted for the GAVA awards and the publication is accurate and factual. All images were provided by the entrants with full cooperation and authorized releases.

Three V Enterprises, GAVA, its representatives, the publishers, and sponsors are not responsible or liable for any misleading or inaccurate data or images contained in this publication.

Library of Congress Control Number: 2009940047

Type set in Futura Std/Zurich BT

ISBN: 978-0-7643-3480-1
Printed in China

Schiffer Books are available at special discounts for bulk purchases for sales promotions or premiums. Special editions, including personalized covers, corporate imprints, and excerpts can be created in large quantities for special needs. For more information contact the publisher:

Published by Schiffer Publishing Ltd.
4880 Lower Valley Road
Atglen, PA 19310
Phone: (610) 593-1777; Fax: (610) 593-2002
E-mail: Info@schifferbooks.com

For the largest selection of fine reference books on this and related subjects, please visit our web site at
www.schifferbooks.com
We are always looking for people to write books on new and related subjects. If you have an idea for a book please contact us at the above address.

This book may be purchased from the publisher.
Include $5.00 for shipping.
Please try your bookstore first.
You may write for a free catalog.

In Europe, Schiffer books are distributed by
Bushwood Books
6 Marksbury Ave.
Kew Gardens
Surrey TW9 4JF England
Phone: 44 (0) 20 8392 8585;
Fax: 44 (0) 20 8392 9876
E-mail: info@bushwoodbooks.co.uk
Website: www.bushwoodbooks.co.uk

CONTENTS

Water fountain at Pueblo Bonito Sunset Beach, Cabo San Lucas. Photo Courtesy of Mary Vail, OSG, Publicist

INTRODUCTION

International Award-Winning Pools, Spas and Water Environments presented by GAVA showcases the most innovative water-inspired design applications from around the globe.

Award winners are artisans, visionaries, and innovators from Australia, Canada, Mexico, the Caribbean, Venezuela, and the United States. After hundreds of inquiries, only 39 earned the prestigious premiere GAVA: Global AquaTekture Visionary Award.

Some designers incorporated tried-and-true methods developed by artisans centuries before, such as an infinity edge. This feature dates back to the fresh-water fountains discovered among the ruins of Pompeii. The application of the overflow design on public fountains kept drinking basins circulating with clean water. In modern times, builders apply the same principle to swimming pools and spas, creating an endless flow of water over the edge, re-circulating back into the pool or spa. Some integrated glass tiles into the design to create intricate mosaics, as found in early European designs.

Ancient stone water fountain unearthed in Pompeii, Italy. The vessel made of four solid slabs of stone, designed with one side set slightly lower, established the water level and overflow. Photo Courtesy of Mary Vail, OSG, Publicist

Others look to new materials to craft their designs. Modern technology provides revolutionary products and powerful tools allowing architects, builders, and designers more freedom, flexibility, and diversity, creating limitless possibilities in design creation. Builders have the ability to craft a rock wall without a single boulder. They can make drastic changes to a design plan within seconds. And clients can review every angle and detail of the project in realistic 3-D.

Water is the common, spectacular element in each of these award-winning projects. Since the beginning of time, mankind has constructed vessels to contain, collect, and divert water; for drinking, cooking, bathing, exercise, therapy, or entertainment. Each becoming an essential and valued element or a gathering place for family, friends, and community members.

Every award-winning design starts with two basic elements: water and the vessel. The distinction comes in how the vessel is designed, shaped, overlaid, divided, enclosed, and equipped.

Modern technology by Structure Studios allows designers such as Jeromey Naugle of Premier Paradise in Chandler, Arizona, to create realistic drawings for clients to review. Screen shot image courtesy of Structure Studios.

GAVA

GAVA recognizes artisans globally whose vision and creativity exemplify the best in *AquaTekture: the discipline of designing, engineering, and erecting of water environments and ancillary components in a harmonious nature with consideration to function, space, and aesthetics.*

GAVA transcends the traditional water-themed design awards by hosting an integrated world-wide competition open to design professionals of all genres dedicated to influencing and creating thought-provoking solutions.

GAVA

GLOBAL **AQUATEKTURE** VISIONARY AWARDS™

THE COMPETITION

The competition acknowledges the most innovative concepts, designs, materials, and applications of water-inspired environments used in commercial, mixed use, hospitality, public use, recreational, and residential venues.

GAVA is the only independent international design awards competition open to all disciplines: architects, contractors, interior and exterior designers, homebuilders, pool builders, landscape architects, and designers.

Categories include pools, spas, water features, lakes, waterfalls, reflection ponds, marine environments, and water fountains. It also includes special materials, such as lighting, acrylic elements, tile, art, natural materials, and green AquaTekture.

As presenting sponsor, Structure Studios bestows a signature award to artisans who used the company's Pool Studio 3-D software to develop their winning concept.

GAVA awards are presented in four levels: gold, silver, bronze, and honorable mention. Gold award winners receive an engraved crystal water drop trophy.

GAVA
GLOBAL AQUATEKTURE VISIONARY AWARDS
Inaugural GAVA Gold Award
2009

Snyder Residence, Las Vegas, Nevada. Photo Courtesy of Mary Vail, OSG, Publicist

RESIDENTIAL AQUATEKTURE

GOLD
AWARD WINNER

Category: Residential Pool All-Tile
Project: Wave On Pool
Cuernavaca, Mexico
Approximately 1000 sf

Mosaicos Venecianos de Mexico/Kolorines

THE VISIONARIES

Mosaicos Venecianos de Mexico/Kolorines *Glass Mosaic Designer and Manufacturer*

Tile Manufacturer: Mosaicos Venecianos de Mexico/Kolorines
Mosaic Manufacturers and Mural Studio
Cuernavaca, Morales, Mexico
01.800.719.9806 Toll free
011.52.777.3296640
www.kolorines.com
Society of American Mosaic Artists
Association of Pool and Spa Professionals

Architect/Designer: Francisco Perdomo, Mosaicos Venecianos

Collaborators: Jose Ventura, contractor
Mosaicos Venecianos de Mexico/Kolorines, mosaic installation

Project Owner: Iniguez Residence

THE VISION

To simulate a seaside ambiance in the backyard pool. Kolorines' design team proposed small generated mosaics that transitioned from blue to tan colors to create a realistic shoreline effect, as if the wave was gently rolling onto the beach.

Features: All-tile interior

Photos Courtesy of Mosaicos Venecianos de Mexico/Kolorines

GOLD AWARDWINNER

POOL

GOLD
AWARD WINNER

Category: Residential Pool All-Tile
Project: Coral Reef Pool
Cuernavaca, Mexico
Approximately 1200 sf

Mosaicos Venecianos de Mexico/Kolorines

THE VISIONARIES

Mosaicos Venecianos de Mexico/Kolorines Glass Mosaic Designer and Manufacturer

Tile Manufacturer: Mosaicos Venecianos de Mexico – Kolorines
Mosaic Manufacturers and Mural Studio
Cuernavaca, Morales, Mexico
01.800.719.9806 Toll free
011.52.777.3296640
www.kolorines.com
Society of American Mosaic Artists
Association of Pool and Spa Professionals

Architect/Designer: Arq. Javier Duarte
A3 Architecture

Collaborators: Arq. Alfonso Abe, contractor
Mosaic Design Kolorines, designers, mosaic installation

Project Owner: Tapia Residence

THE VISION

To create an elaborate life-like coral reef within the interior of the pool. As the mosaic manufacturer and mural studio, Kolorines provided its expertise in the interior pool mosaics of the project. Computer generated mosaic corals were mixed with highly detailed hand-made mosaics to give a realistic marine environment appearance. The highly detailed and elaborate scene showcases a variety of corals, fish and turtles.

Features: All-tile interior

Photos Courtesy of Mosaicos Venecianos de Mexico/Kolorines

GOLD AWARDWINNER

POOL

GOLD
AWARDWINNER

Category: Residential Pool Geometric
Project: Dynamic Modernism
Las Vegas, Nevada, USA
Pool 426 sf Spa 89 sf

Attanasio Landscape Architect

THE VISIONARIES

Attanasio Landscape Architect Designer

Designer:	Chris Attanasio, ASLA Principal Attanasio Landscape Architect Las Vegas, Nevada, USA 702.255.7160 www.ala-lv.com American Society of Landscape Architects
Collaborators:	Paragon Pools, contractor www.paragonpools.net
Project Owner:	Jonathan Meyers

THE VISION

The Vision of Dynamic Modernism was to combine contrasting colors, refined textures and bold finishes, to create a contemporary design within an extremely narrow space. The sharp geometric lines of the pool and raised spa craft an intriguing impression against the curved, elevated water feature and seating bench and the ground level, multi-sized landscape balls. A raised linear fire element parallels the pool, adding flashes of color and gentle warmth.

Features:	Structure Studios Pool Studio 3-D Design Zodiac Pool Systems/Jandy Equipment Paramount Pool & Spa Systems In-floor cleaner

Photos Courtesy of Mary Vail, OSG Publicist

GOLD AWARDWINNER

POOL

GOLD AWARDWINNER

Category: Residential Pool Geometric
Project: Kamel
Mission, Texas, USA
425 sf

Euro Pools, LLC

THE VISIONARIES

Euro Pools, LLC

Designer: Euro Pools, LLC
McAllen, Texas, USA
956.631.1301
www.euro-pools.com
Association of Pool and Spa Professionals

Collaborators: R. Sanchez
Maxal Construction

Project Owner: Lourdes Godinez

THE VISION

To create a dramatic contemporary pool, spa and water feature that would complement the home from diverse angles. The pool becomes an extension of the house structure with a water feature that flows from a curved architectural arch. LED lights heighten the drama of the setting.

Features: Triangle shaped raised spa

Photos Courtesy of Euro Pools, LLC

GOLD AWARD WINNER

POOL

GOLD
AWARD WINNER

Category: Residential Pool Traditional
Project: Boulder Ridge – Christopher Homes Model Pool
Las Vegas, Nevada, USA
597 sf

Robert Stone, Nuvis Landscape Architect & Planning

THE VISIONARIES

Robert Stone, Nuvis Landscape Architect & Planning

Designer:
Robert Stone, ASLA
Nuvis Landscape Architect & Planning
Costa Mesa, California, USA
714.754.7311
www.nuvis.net
American Society of Landscape Architects

Collaborators:
Paragon Pools, contractor
www.paragonpools.net

Project Owner:
Christopher Homes
www.christopherhomes.com

THE VISION

To design a showcase model pool for a luxury home development. Utilizing the steep slope and necessary retaining wall, an elaborate water feature with cascading troughs of water in bold copper tapered forms spills down the stone wall, past planters on raised stone pilasters.

Features:
Zodiac Pool Systems/Jandy Equipment
Paramount Pool & Spa Systems In-floor cleaner

Photos Courtesy of Mary Vail, OSG Publicist

GOLD AWARDWINNER | POOL

SILVOR
AWARD WINNER

Category: Residential Pool Traditional
Project: Davis Residence
Augusta, Georgia, USA
650 sf

Indigo Pool and Spa, Inc.

THE VISIONARIES

Indigo Pool and Spa, Inc. Designer/Builder

Designer:

Blair Brown
Indigo Pool and Spa, Inc.
Greensboro, Georgia, USA
706.999.1413
www.indigopoolandspa.com
Association of Pool and Spa Professionals
National Association of Home Builders
Aquatech Society

Project Owner: Davis Residence

THE VISION

To incorporate an elevated all-tile perimeter overflow spa within a classic Roman style pool. Precise and accurate tile placement allowed for a seamless flow of water over the edges. Custom blended glass tile and deck jets add sophisticated touches to the overall look.

Features:

Structure Studios Pool Studio 3-D Design
Zodiac Pool Systems/Jandy Equipment
Paramount Pool & Spa Systems In-floor cleaner

Photos Courtesy of Blair Brown

SILVOR AWARDWINNER

POOL

GOLD AWARD WINNER

Category: Residential Pool Freeform
Project: Johnson Residence
Peoria, Arizona, USA
Pool 214 perimeter, Spa 30 perimeter

Cameo Pools

THE VISIONARIES

Cameo Pools Designer/Builder

Designer: Larry Duffy
Cameo Pools
Mesa, Arizona, USA
480.969.4034
www.cameopools.com
Aquatech Society of Pool Builders
Southwest Pool and Spa Association

Project Owner: Johnson Residence

THE VISION

To design a resort setting complete with grotto, slide with swim through cave, combination natural and man-made waterfall with fire elements, swim-up bar, tanning area, and flyover bridge. Additional water features from the roof line of the bar and bridge bring movement and theatrics to the pool.

Features: Zodiac Pool Systems/Jandy Equipment
Paramount Pool & Spa Systems In-floor cleaner

Photos Courtesy of Cameo Pools

GOLD AWARDWINNER | POOL

SILVOR
AWARDWINNER

Category: Residential Pool Freeform
Project: LaMothe Residence
Evans, Georgia, USA
875 sf

Indigo Pool and Spa, Inc.

THE VISIONARIES

Indigo Pool and Spa, Inc. Contractor

Designers: Roger Davis
Davis Design Group
Blair Brown
Indigo Pool & Spa, Inc.

Contractor: Indigo Pool and Spa, Inc.
Greensboro, Georgia, USA
706.999.1413
www.indigopoolandspa.com
Association of Pool and Spa Professionals
National Association of Home Builders
Aquatech Society

Project Owner: LaMothe Residence

THE VISION

To re-create a natural boulder waterfall for the centerpiece of the outdoor entertainment experience. Rising two-stories high, a crane was utilized for precise placement of the boulders. A seventeen foot slide and large wet deck add playful dimensions to the setting.

Features: Structure Studios Pool Studio 3-D Design
Zodiac Pool Systems/Jandy Equipment
Paramount Pool & Spa Systems In-floor cleaner

Photos Courtesy of James P. Brown

SILVOR
AWARDWINNER

POOL

GOLD AWARDWINNER

Category: Residential Pool Natural Setting
Project: Villa Capacious
Las Vegas, Nevada, USA
66,000 gallons

Sun West Custom Homes

THE VISIONARIES

Sun West Custom Homes Designer/Builder

Designer: Daniel S. Coletti
Sun West Custom Homes
Las Vegas, Nevada, USA
702.363.8060
www.sunwestcustomhomes.com

Project Owner: Wattles Residence

THE VISION

To inspire fun in a multi-level water wonderland with three waterfalls, underwater speakers, a slide, swing, grotto, diving board, diving platform, and water volleyball.

Photos Courtesy of Sun West Custom Homes

GOLD AWARD WINNER | POOL

BRONZE
AWARDWINNER

Category: Residential Pool Natural Setting
Project: Ruzika Residence
Greensboro, Georgia, USA
615 sf

Indigo Pool and Spa, Inc.

THE VISIONARIES

Indigo Pool and Spa, Inc. Contractor

Designer: Lynn Mills & Amy Oglesby
Miller Brown Family Companies

Contractor: Indigo Pool and Spa, Inc.
Greensboro, Georgia, USA
706.999.1413
www.indigopoolandspa.com
Association of Pool and Spa Professionals
National Association of Home Builders
Aquatech Society

Project Owner: Ruzika Residence

THE VISION

To design a pool, spa combination on this shoreline property that escapes from the norm. The result is an elevated pool that spills over a natural stone waterfall into an oversized spa. To minimize the visual impact of the natural environment a custom underground vault houses one hundred percent of the equipment. This property boasts an entertainment area, fireplace, and customized PGA-approved putting green.

Features: Structure Studios Pool Studio 3-D Design
Zodiac Pool Systems/Jandy Equipment
Paramount Pool & Spa Systems In-floor cleaner

Photos Courtesy of James P. Brown

BRONZE AWARD WINNER | POOL

GOLD
AWARDWINNER

Category: Infinity Pool
Project: Snyder Residence
Las Vegas, Nevada, USA
17′ x 52′ x 6′

Robert Stone, Nuvis Landscape Architect & Planning

THE VISIONARIES

Robert Stone, Nuvis Landscape Architect & Planning

Designer: Robert Stone, ASLA
Nuvis Landscape Architect & Planning
Costa Mesa, California, USA
714.754.7311
www.nuvis.net
American Society of Landscape Architects

Collaborators: Paragon Pools, contractor
www.paragonpools.net

Project Owner: Snyder Residence

THE VISION

To design a pool that does not intrude on the sweeping, unobstructed mountain and desert views but rather enhances the visual appeal. Positioning the low profile, infinity pool at the edge of the vast property expands the beauty of the natural terrain with a reflection pond effect.

Features: Zodiac Pool Systems/Jandy Equipment
Paramount Pool & Spa Systems In-floor cleaner

Photos Courtesy of Mary Vail, OSG Publicist

GOLD AWARD WINNER | POOL

GOLD
AWARD WINNER

Category: Residential Infinity Pool
Project: Grubb Residence
Greensboro, Georgia, USA
770 sf

Indigo Pool and Spa, Inc.

THE VISIONARIES

Indigo Pool and Spa, Inc. Designer-Builder

Designer: Blair Brown
Indigo Pool and Spa, Inc.
Greensboro, Georgia, USA
706.999.1413
www.indigopoolandspa.com
Association of Pool and Spa Professionals
National Association of Home Builders
Aquatech Society

Project Owner: Grubb Residence

THE VISION

To design a seamless infinity pool and entertainment venue enhancing the view and ambiance of the lakeside residence. Special construction engineering was required to accommodate for the extreme slope of the property. The pool is highlighted with natural stone, fire bowls, and colored lighting.

Features: Structure Studios Pool Studio 3-D Design
Zodiac Pool Systems/Jandy Equipment
Paramount Pool & Spa Systems In-floor cleaner

Photos Courtesy of Blair Brown

GOLD AWARD WINNER

POOL

BRONZE
AWARDWINNER

Category: Residential Infinity Pool
Project: Green Residence
Las Vegas, Nevada, USA
40 ft x 28 ft

Tannie's Design Works & Paragon Pools

THE VISIONARIES

Tannie's Design Works & Paragon Pools Designers

Designers:

Tannie Luke
Tannie's Design Works
702.252.7355
Las Vegas, Nevada, USA
www.tannieluke.com

Bill Sachanko
Paragon Pools
Las Vegas, Nevada, USA
www.paragonpools.com

Collaborators:

Richard Luke Architects, architect
www.richardlukearchitects.com

Paragon Pools, contractor

Project Owner: Green Residence

THE VISION

To create a functional pool with a contemporary look. The location of the elevated spa and the large infinity edge capitalize on the slope of the lot as well as the mountain and city views. The addition of a curved weeping wall provides an extra water element to the setting.

Features:

Structure Studios Pool Studio 3-D Design
Zodiac Pool Systems/Jandy Equipment
Paramount Pool & Spa Systems In-floor cleaner

Photos Courtesy of Mary Vail, OSG Publicist

BRONZE
AWARDWINNER

POOL

GOLD
AWARD WINNER

Category: Residential Perimeter Slot Pool
Project: Guerrero Residence
Valencia, Venezuela
672 sf

Edwin Vives, Venezolana de Piscinas

THE VISIONARIES

Edwin Vives, Venezolana de Piscinas Designer/Builder

Designer: Edwin Vives
Venezolana de Piscinas
Valencia, Venezuela
58.241.826.42.62
www.venezolanadepiscinas.com

Project Owner: Guerrero Residence

THE VISION

To design a visually relaxing environment. The perimeter slot pool adds a calm reflective quality to complement the contemporary architecture of the residence.

Features: Deck Jet Laminars
Fiber Optics

Photos Courtesy of Edwin Vives

GOLD AWARD WINNER

POOL

GOLD
AWARDWINNER

Category: Residential Pool "Green" Environmentally Friendly
Project: O'Hare Residence
Samford, Queensland, Australia
16.6m x 5m

Stuart Bevan Pools Pty. Ltd.

THE VISIONARIES

Stuart Bevan Pools Pty. Ltd. Designer/Builder

Designer: Stuart Bevan
Stuart Bevan Pools Pty. Ltd.
Red Hill, Queensland, Australia
07.33664444
www.stuartbevanpools.com.au
Queensland Master Builders Association

Project Owner: O'Hare Residence

THE VISION

Create a unique space with multi-facets in mind: to complement the surrounding natural rural beauty, to minimize the impact on the environment, to develop daily and long term sustainability, and to expound on the majestic views. Constructing this pool, extending over a steep embankment and rising approximately thirteen meters from ground-to-tip required considerable engineering and landscape contouring to prevent damage from high-winds or land corrosion from severe storms. Water conservation components include: potable water tanks for pool and landscape needs, a dedicated catchment tank under the deck for excess rainwater overflow, and a recycling system for sand filter backwash.

Features: All-tile interior
Timber deck
Paramount Pool & Spa Systems In-floor cleaner
Electric heat pump and solar blanket

Photos Courtesy of Stuart Bevan

GOLD AWARDWINNER

POOL

SILVOR
AWARDWINNER

Category: Residential Pool Renovation
Project: Capper Remodel
Dallas, Texas, USA
60 ft x 25 ft

Craig Cameron, Natural Water Environments

THE VISIONARIES

Craig Cameron Natural Water Environments

Designers:

Craig Cameron
Natural Water Environments
Dallas, Texas, USA
817.905.7343
www.natural-water-env.com

Gideon Toal Architecture
Dallas, Texas, USA
817.335.4991
www.gideontoal.com

Collaborators:

Craig Cameron, contractor
Frank W. Neal & Associates, engineer
Landmark Construction, wood work

Project Owner: Capper Residence

THE VISION

Save the pool! This classic, large rectangle pool with spring diving board on a Fort Worth hillside was destined for doom after mud slides caused major damaged to the integrity of the structure. As part of the renovation process, major structural repair and engineering was required to stabilize and level the 12.5 feet deep pool including adding eighteen 16-inch piers up to twenty-four feet deep tied together with an 18x18 inch beam on the hillside, excavating 360 degrees around the pool, core drilled new plumbing, adding three skimmers, four new main drains, and in-floor pool returns for increased efficiency, jack hammering out structural cracks in the floor and walls, adding steel reinforcements, and re-leveling the pool beam by raising it as much as ten inches in some sections and adding step-out and thirty feet of seating inside the pool as well as an automatic pool cover. To complicate the situation, the steep limited access of the site presented additional problems.

Features:

IPE wood deck inserts, custom benches and tables
Sheer descent
Firepit and sitting area
Two-toned concrete deck
Raised lounging area
Zodiac Pool Systems/Jandy Equipment

Photos Courtesy of Craig Cameron

SILVOR AWARDWINNER

POOL

AFTER

EFORE

GOLD
AWARDWINNER

Category: Structure Studios - Pool Studio 3D Design Award
Project: Davidson Residence
Redlands, California, USA
37 ft x 20 ft

Islander Pools

THE VISIONARIES

Islander Pools Designer/Builder

Designer: Frank Himpelmann
Islander Pools
Riverside, California, USA
951.354.9888
www.islanderpools.net

Project Owner: Davidson Residence

THE VISION

To create a grand entry for a five-acre estate. The project was inspired by the location of the home on the property. In addition to taking advantage of the view from deck and interior of the natural stone and boulder infinity pool, detail was given to the spillway and trough creating a stunning visual for those approaching the residence.

Utilizing the Structure Studio Pool Studio 3D design program we were able to convey to the client the concept drawing for this dramatic pool with precise and realistic detail, granting him a view from every angle. The homeowner accepted the design on its initial draft without any changes. He was amazed how exact the completed project was in comparison to the original 3D design.

Features: Structure Studios Pool Studio 3-D design
Paramount Pool & Spa Systems In-floor cleaner

Photos Courtesy of Hagan Photography

GOLD AWARDWINNER

POOL

GOLD
AWARD WINNER

Category: Residential Pool Special Materials (Aqua Sphere)
Project: Club Point
Las Vegas, Nevada, USA
48,864 gallons

Sun West Custom Homes

THE VISIONARIES

Sun West Custom Homes Designer/Builder

Designer:

Daniel S. Coletti
Sun West Custom Homes
Las Vegas, Nevada, USA
702.363.8060
www.sunwestcustomhomes.com

Project Owner: Menzies Residence

THE VISION

Old world themed infinity pool with touch of modern day technology. For a dramatic entry statement, a thirty inch acrylic Aqua Sphere is suspended on the water. The acrylic ball resting atop an acrylic tube fills with water when activated, the water then gently flows through a hole in the top of the sphere spilling over the outside of the ball. Additionally, the sphere is lighted from below.

Features:

Floating firepit with pop-up television
Acrylic sphere
www.waterfountains.com/fountain.html
Raised spa

Photos Courtesy of Sun West Custom Homes

GOLD AWARD WINNER | POOL

GOLD
AWARDWINNER

Category: Residential Pool Special Materials (Acrylic Panel)
Project: Liquid Window
Las Vegas, Nevada, USA
Upper pool 11ft x 28 ft, Lower pool 14 ft x 44 ft

ATM – Acrylic Tank Manufacturing

THE VISIONARIES

ATM – Acrylic Tank Manufacturing

Designer: Joe Vassallo, CBP
Joe Vassallo, Jr. CBP
Paragon Pools

Acrylic Manufacturer: ATM
Las Vegas, Nevada, USA
877.826.5286
www.acrylicaquariums.com

Collaborators: Paragon Pools, contractor
www.paragonpools.net

Project Owner: Vassallo Residence

THE VISION

To create a unique infinity design incorporating an acrylic panel to separate the multi-level pool, simulating water suspended in space. Engineering criteria for the fourteen foot acrylic piece required the panel to be three inches thick. A crane was utilized to lower the 1,400 pound acrylic panel into specially constructed channels.

Features: Structure Studios Pool Studio 3-D Design
Zodiac Pool Systems/Jandy Equipment
Paramount Pool & Spa Systems In-floor cleaner

Photos Courtesy of Mary Vail, OSG Publicist

GOLD AWARD WINNER

POOL

GOLD
AWARDWINNER

Category: Residential Pool * Fire
Projects: Earth Elements
Las Vegas, Nevada, USA
470 sf

Tannie's Design Works

THE VISIONARIES

Tannie's Design Works

Designer: Tannie Luke
Tannie's Design Works
702.252.7355
Las Vegas, Nevada, USA
www.tannieluke.com

Collaborators: Richard Luke Architects
www.richardlukearchitects.com

Paragon Pools, contractor
www.paragonpools.net

Project Owner: Luke Residence

THE VISION

To create multiple quaint, intimate, entertaining spaces utilizing a Feng Shui-inspired environment with fire, water, pebbles, and other natural elements in a small space. Large poolside sitting rocks are fashioned with custom cushions. The setting is completed by adding a mix of desert and tropical foliage.

Features: Structure Studios Pool Studio 3-D Design
Zodiac Pool Systems/Jandy Equipment
Paramount Pool & Spa Systems In-floor cleaner

Photos Courtesy of Mary Vail, OSG Publicist

GOLD AWARDWINNER

POOL

GOLD AWARDWINNER

Category: Residential Spa
Project: Penthouse Swim-spa
Dallas, Texas, USA
8 ft x 19 ft

Craig Cameron, Natural Water Environments

THE VISIONARIES

Craig Cameron Natural Water Environments

Designers: Craig Cameron
Natural Water Environments
Dallas, Texas, USA
817.905.7343
www.natural-water-env.com

Workarchitecture
Dallas, Texas, USA

Collaborators: Craig Cameron, contractor
Bradford Products
Xavier Zamarripa, artist

Project Owner: Winspear Residence

THE VISION

To create a room that reflects the picturesque scenery of the client's boyhood countryside in the Canadian Rockies within the eighteenth floor of his Dallas penthouse. Resonating the sights and sounds of the mountains, a thirteen-foot negative edge drops six feet into a catch basin filled with life-size Canadian trout sculptures. A tile mosaic wall mural and a vine sculpted curved staircase and railings add the final touches to complete the setting.

Constructing the project within the penthouse created numerous challenges requiring special engineering and detailed planning such as craning pre-built sections into the penthouse window, adding self-leveling shock absorbers, and under-structure water alarm sensors.

Features: Custom Venetian glass tile
Swim spa exercise unit

Photos Courtesy of Craig Cameron

GOLD AWARDWINNER

SPA

SILVOR
AWARDWINNER

Category: Residential Spa
Project: Snyder Residence
Las Vegas, Nevada, USA
13 ft x 7.5 ft

Robert Stone, Nuvis Landscape Architect & Planning

THE VISIONARIES

Robert Stone Nuvis Landscape Architect & Planning

Designer: Robert Stone, ASLA
Nuvis Landscape Architect & Planning
Costa Mesa, California, USA
714.754.7311
www.nuvis.net
American Society of Landscape Architects

Collaborators: Paragon Pools, contractor
www.paragonpools.net

Project Owner: Snyder Residence

THE VISION

Design a private, sanctuary spa to compliment the architecture of the home as well as the other water elements in the atypical shaped lot. In close proximately to the master suite, the elevated spa was situated adjacent to a large retaining wall offering seclusion and privacy from neighboring homes. Blending with the fountain and pool design, slate tiles were incorporated on the spa exterior and spillway.

Features: Zodiac Pool Systems/Jandy Equipment
Paramount Pool & Spa Systems In-floor cleaner

Photos Courtesy of Mary Vail, OSG Publicist

SILVOR AWARDWINNER

SPA

GOLD AWARD WINNER

Category: Residential Spa All-Tile
Project: Casita Spa
Las Vegas, Nevada, USA
294 sf

Dal-tile Corporation

THE VISIONARIES

Dal-tile Corporation

Designer:	Joe Vassallo, CBP Joe Vassallo, Jr. CBP Paragon Pools www.paragonpools.net
Tile Distributor:	Dal-tile Corporation Dallas, Texas, USA 214.398.1411 www.daltile.com
Collaborators:	Paragon Pools, contractor
Project Owner:	Vassallo Residence

THE VISION

To design an old world inspired, oversized enclosed spa for year round comfort. One inch square Caribbean surf blend tiles provide contrasting hues against the earth tone faux enclosure and paver stone decking. Agassi-Graf patio collection furnishings by Kreiss and a large flat screen TV add a touch of modern flair to the setting.

Features:	Structure Studios Pool Studio 3-D Design Zodiac Pool Systems/Jandy Equipment Paramount Pool & Spa Systems In-floor cleaner Built in fireplace

Photos Courtesy of Mary Vail, OSG Publicist

GOLD AWARDWINNER | SPA

GOLD AWARDWINNER

Category: Residential Water feature * Fire
Project: Water & Fire in Suspension
Oakville, Ontario, Canada
170 sf

International Landscaping, Inc.

THE VISIONARIES

International Landscaping, Inc. Landscape Architect/Contractor

Designer/Contractor: Jay Jackson
International Landscaping, Inc.
Ontario, Canada
905.876.3000
www.internationallandscaping.com
Member Landscape Ontario

THE VISION

Design an architectural water and fire feature into an intimate courtyard sanctuary. The setting, visible from many vantage points on the property provides year-round enjoyment. Asian and art inspired elements celebrate the lifestyle of the homeowners. Positioned in the core of the dual spillover stone waterfall, the raised fire pit seems to defy gravity.

Features: Stainless steel curtain style sheer descent
Carved stone sculpture

Photos Courtesy of International Landscaping, Inc.

GOLD AWARD WINNER | WATER FEATURE

GOLD
AWARDWINNER

Category: Residential Water feature * Art
Project: Snyder Residence
Las Vegas, Nevada, USA
113 sf

Robert Stone, Nuvis Landscape Architect & Planning

THE VISIONARIES

Robert Stone Nuvis Landscape Architect & Planning

Designer:	Robert Stone, ASLA Nuvis Landscape Architect & Planning Costa Mesa, California, USA 714.754.7311 www.nuvis.net American Society of Landscape Architects
Collaborators:	Paragon Pools, contractor www.paragonpools.net
Project Owner:	Snyder Residence

THE VISION

Create a sculpture accent water feature without infringing on the mountain and desert valley views. Drawing one's attention away from a large retaining wall, a sculpture is situated in the midst of an elevated, pie-shaped, duel spilling water feature with stainless steel weirs. The jubilation of the young fisherman with his catch brings an animated spirit to the fountain and backyard setting.

Features: Zodiac Pool Systems/Jandy Equipment

Photos Courtesy of Mary Vail, OSG Publicist

GOLD AWARDWINNER | WATER FEATURE

GOLD
AWARDWINNER

Category: Residential Art
Project: Glassic Mirage Waterfall
Las Vegas, Nevada, USA
Various sizes

Leslie Rankin, Glassic Art

THE VISIONARIES

Leslie Rankin Glassic Art

Designer/Artist: Leslie Rankin
Glassic Art
Las Vegas, Nevada, USA
888.834.1639
www.glassicart.com

THE VISION

The goal was to create waterless, waterfall-like glass sculptures. Undulating custom-made glass pieces give the illusion of water flowing. Years of research and development, these ecology minded pieces generate a stunning visual effect while saving water and energy resources. Placed adjacent to this pool, the three Glassic Art pieces creates the appearance of elongated sheets of water trickling towards the pool.

Photos Courtesy of Mary Vail, OSG Photography

GOLD AWARDWINNER

SPECIAL APPLICATION

Jade Mountain, St. Lucia, Caribbean. Photo Courtesy of Jade Mountain

COMMERCIAL AQUATEKTURE

GOLD
AWARD WINNER

Category: Commercial Pool Resort All-Tile
Project: Iberostar Grand Paraiso
Riviera Maya, Mexico
Approximately 7000 sf

Mosaicos Venecianos de Mexico/Kolorines

THE VISIONARIES

Mosaicos Venecianos de Mexico/Kolorines Glass Mosaic Manufacturer & Designer

Tile Manufacturer: Mosaicos Venecianos de Mexico – Kolorines
Mosaic Manufacturers and Mural Studio
Cuernavaca, Morales, Mexico
01.800.719.9806
011.52.777.3296640
www.kolorines.com
Society of American Mosaic Artists
Association of Pool and Spa Professionals

Architect/Designer: Miriam Panduro
Iberostar Hotel and Resorts

Collaborators: Arq. Deudero, contractor

Project Owner: Iberostar Hotels
www.iberostar.com

THE VISION

In harmony with the Classic Italian Architecture of the hotel, the expansive all-tile pool with multiple spas, large lounging wet decks, floating fountains, swim-up bar, and accent mosaics reflect the blue and green hues of the sea.

Photos Courtesy of Iberostar Hotel and Resorts

GOLD AWARDWINNER

POOL

SILVOR
AWARD WINNER

Category: Commercial Pool Resort All-Tile
Project: Hilton Villahermosa
Villahermosa, Tab. Mexico
Approximately 8000 sf

Mosaicos Venecianos de Mexico/Kolorines

THE VISIONARIES

Mosaicos Venecianos de Mexico/Kolorines Glass Mosaic Manufacturer & Designer

Tile Manufacturer: Mosaicos Venecianos de Mexico – Kolorines
Mosaic Manufacturers and Mural Studio
Cuernavaca, Morales, Mexico
01.800.719.9806
011.52.777.3296640
www.kolorines.com
Society of American Mosaic Artists
Association of Pool and Spa Professionals

Architect/Designer: Arq. Gomez Cano/Dino Valezzi

Collaborators: Arango Pools, contractor

Project Owner: Hilton Hotels
1.800.445.8667
www.hiltonhotels.com

THE VISION

Complementing the surrounding esthetics, the interior mosaics design of the all-tile, multi-level pool and spa graduate from light crème tones to deep rich blues accentuating the varying depths.

Photos Courtesy of Hilton Hotels and Mosaicos Venecianos de Mexico/Kolorines

SILVOR AWARDWINNER | POOL

BRONZE
AWARDWINNER

Category: Commercial Pool Resort All-Tile
Project: Banyan Tree Mayakoba Resort
Riviera Maya, Mexico
Approximately 5000 sf

Mosaicos Venecianos de Mexico/Kolorines

THE VISIONARIES

Mosaicos Venecianos de Mexico/Kolorines Glass Mosaic Manufacturer & Designer

Tile Manufacturer: Mosaicos Venecianos de Mexico – Kolorines
Mosaic Manufacturers and Mural Studio
Cuernavaca, Morales, Mexico
01.800.719.9806
011.52.777.3296640
www.kolorines.com
Society of American Mosaic Artists
Association of Pool and Spa Professionals

Architect/Designer: Mario Lazo/Dino Valezzi
Unidad de Diseno/Kolorines

Collaborators: OHL, contractor
Mosaicos Venecianos de Mexico - Kolorines, mosaic installation

Project Owner: Banyan Tree Resorts
www.banyantree.com

THE VISION

Surrounded by beautiful natural landscaping, water channels were designed around the property with minimal impact to the habitat. The vision of the freeform resort pool was to create an iridescent, white sand interior that followed the design criteria.

Photos Courtesy of Mosaicos Venecianos de Mexico/Kolorines

BRONZE
AWARDWINNER

POOL

GOLD
AWARDWINNER

Category: Commercial Resort Infinity Pool
Project: Jade Mountain Infinity Pools
St. Lucia, Caribbean
Multiple pools range from 400 to 900 sf

Jade Mountain

THE VISIONARIES

Jade Mountain

Architect/Contractor: Nick Troubetzkoy
Nick Troubetzkoy Architect and Planners

Project Owner: Nick Troubetzkoy
Jade Mountain
St. Lucia
800.223.1108 US
0.800.894.057 UK
www.jademountain.com

THE VISION

To develop spaces and experiences giving guests an ethereal, spiritual lift. Every sanctuary of the resort has its own infinity pool, allowing one to breathe and bathe freely in complete privacy while being intimately connected with the environment.

To expand on the architect's philosophy of designing and building in harmony with the Caribbean, creating a mesmerizing resort experience. The bold architectural design includes individual bridges leading to exceptional multiple infinity pool sanctuaries and rugged stoned-faced columns reaching toward the sky.

Primary elements of the building's design, each pool is unique both in colour and shape, serving as organic components in each suite, as well as in the building as a whole. The all-tile pools were made completely with recycled glass tile, which was repetitively layered, folded, fired, and re-fired in a method similar to that used to create Damascus steel blades, creating the effect of an iridescent Persian carpet.

Features: Recycled glass tile

Photos Courtesy of Jade Mountain

GOLD AWARD WINNER

POOL

BRONZE AWARD WINNER

Category: Commercial Resort Infinity Pool
Project: Villa Pools at the Montecristo * Pueblo Bonito Oceanfront Resorts and Spas
Cabo San Lucas, Baja California Sur
Multiple pools vary in size

Montecristo

THE VISIONARIES

Montecristo Pueblo Bonito Oceanfront Resorts and Spas

Architect/Designer: Arq. Anthony Mullen

Collaborators: Cotur, contractor

Project Owner: Ernesto Coppel
Pueblo Bonito Oceanfront Resorts and Spas
Cabo San Lucas, Baja California Sur
800.990.8250
www.pueblobonito.com

THE VISION

Create a series of exquisite, intimate pools attached to private villas. Overlooking the breathtaking Baja California Sur peninsula, where the Sea of Cortez meets the Pacific Ocean, eighty-two villas are carved into the mountainside rising 350 meters. Blue tile interior mimics the ocean, while earth tone tiles and natural stone on the infinity dam walls allow the pools to blend with the natural desert landscape.

Features: All-tile pools

Photos Courtesy of Mary Vail, OSG Publicist

BRONZE AWARDWINNER

POOL

SILVOR
AWARDWINNER

Category: Commercial Pool Multi-use
Project: Mosaic Loft
McAllen, Texas, USA
900 sf

Euro Pools, LLC

THE VISIONARIES

Euro Pools, LLC

Designer:
Euro Pools, LLC
McAllen, Texas, USA
956.631.1303
www.euro-pools.com
Association of Pool and Spa Professionals

Rafael Sanchez
Maxal Construction

Project Owner:
Mosaic Apartments and Lofts
McAllen, Texas
www.mosaiclofts.com

THE VISION

To create a pool, spa, and fountain complementing the cool, urban, modern architecture of the apartment/lofts. Playing off the name of the property, bold colored tiles were incorporated to make dramatic statements accenting selected spaces in the pool and spa including the built-in wet deck lounge chairs, fountain, and oversized spa.

Photos Courtesy of Euro Pools, LLC

SILVOR AWARDWINNER

POOL

SILVOR
AWARDWINNER

Category: Commercial Pool Waterpark
Project: Bill and Lillie Heinrich YMCA Waterpark
Las Vegas, Nevada, USA
Total lap, activity, and slide pools: 23,000 gallons

Bill and Lillie Heinrich YMCA

THE VISIONARIES

Bill and Lillie Heinrich YMCA

Architect/Designer: JMA
702.731.2033
www.jmaarch.com

Collaborators: Martin Harris Construction, general contractor
www.martinharris.com

Project Owner: Bill and Lillie Heinrich YMCA
702.877.9622
www.lasvegasymca.org

THE VISION

Create a fun and interactive water entertainment venue for members and guests of all ages. Multiple bodies of water were designed to accommodate the varying needs of the organization's activities, programs, and members.

Features: Waterslide – 45 ft tall, 55 ft long
Lap pool – 25 yards, 3 wide lanes
Activity area – play structure, water curtain, dump buckets
Lounge area

Photos Courtesy of Mary B. Vail, OSG Photographer

SILVOR AWARDWINNER

POOL

SILVOR
AWARDWINNER

Category: Commercial Resort Spa
Project: Spa at Sunset Beach * Pueblo Bonito Oceanfront Resorts and Spas
Cabo San Lucas, Baja California Sur
Hot tub 1,585 gallons, cold plunge 200 gallons

Pueblo Bonito Sunset Beach

THE VISIONARIES

Pueblo Bonito Sunset Beach
Pueblo Bonito Oceanfront Resorts and Spas

Architect/Designer: Mizrain Corpus
Pueblo Bonito Oceanfront Resorts and Spas

Collaborators: Cotur, contractor

Project Owner: Ernesto Coppel
Pueblo Bonito Oceanfront Resorts and Spas
Cabo San Lucas, Baja California Sur
800.990.8250
www.pueblobonito.com

THE VISION

To enhance the Spa's wet area experience. Contrasting water environments with an elevated hot tub and step-down submersible cold plunge therapy pools are situated at opposing ends of the spacious lounge area. Modern Mexican architecture features quarry stone, iridescent tiles, wall sconces, columns, and an arched ceiling.

Features: All-tile interior
Zodiac Pool Systems/Jandy Equipment

Photos Courtesy of Mary Vail, OSG Publicist

SILVOR AWARDWINNER

SPA

BRONZE
AWARDWINNER

Category: Commercial Resort Spa
Project: Armonia Spa, Pueblo Bonito Pacifica Holistic Retreat & Spa
Cabo San Lucas, Baja California Sur
Hot tub 657 gallons & Cold plunge 657 gallons

Pueblo Bonito Pacifica Holistic Retreat & Spa

THE VISIONARIES

Pueblo Bonito Pacifica Holistic Retreat & Spa
Pueblo Bonito Oceanfront Resorts and Spas

Architect/Designer: Mizrain Corpus
Pueblo Bonito Oceanfront Resorts and Spas

Collaborators: Cotur, contractor

Project Owner: Ernesto Coppel
Pueblo Bonito Oceanfront Resorts and Spas
Cabo San Lucas, Baja California Sur
800.990.8250
www.pueblobonito.com

THE VISION

Design a peaceful, Zen-inspired sanctuary dedicated to total wellness, guided by the holistic theme of treating body, mind, and spirit as one. In harmony with natural elements, the elevated side-by-side hot tub and cold plunge are crafted with sand excavated from the local beach. The minimal, serene décor is lightly accented with simplistic black and white mosaic tile walls.

Features: Zodiac Pool Systems/Jandy Equipment

Photos Courtesy of Mary Vail, OSG Publicist

BRONZE AWARDWINNER

SPA

SILVOR
AWARDWINNER

Category: Commercial Resort Spa (Pre-fabricated Hot-Tub)
Project: Couples Room in the Armonia Spa,
Pueblo Bonito Pacifica Holistic Retreat & Spa
Cabo San Lucas, Baja California Sur

Pueblo Bonito Pacifica Holistic Retreat & Spa, Pueblo Bonito Oceanfront Resorts and Spas

THE VISIONARIES

Pueblo Bonito Pacifica Holistic Retreat & Spa
Pueblo Bonito Oceanfront Resorts and Spas

Architect/Designer:	Mizrain Corpus Pueblo Bonito Oceanfront Resorts and Spas
Collaborators:	Cotur, contractor
Project Owner:	Ernesto Coppel Pueblo Bonito Oceanfront Resorts and Spas Cabo San Lucas, Baja California Sur 800.990.8250 www.pueblobonito.com

THE VISION

Design an intimate, private setting ideal for couples to enjoy a complete spa experience together, from simultaneous massage treatments to wet therapy in a Zen-inspired setting. An elevated therapeutic hot tub encased in wood slats is positioned between the steam and sauna rooms. Floor-to-ceiling black and white tiles with mosaic designs complement the elegant simplicity of the décor.

Photos Courtesy of Mary Vail, OSG Publicist

SILVOR AWARDWINNER | SPA

GOLD
AWARDWINNER

Category: Commercial Water feature
Project: Veranda Water feature * Pueblo Bonito Pacifica Holistic Retreat & Spa
Cabo San Lucas, Baja California Sur
Spanning over 90 ft

Pueblo Bonito Pacifica Holistic Retreat & Spa, Pueblo Bonito Oceanfront Resorts and Spas

THE VISIONARIES

Pueblo Bonito Pacifica Holistic Retreat & Spa
Pueblo Bonito Oceanfront Resorts and Spas

Architect/Designer: Arq. Fernando Molins
Molins Arquitectos
www.molinsarquitectos.com

Collaborators: Cotur, contractor

Project Owner: Ernesto Coppel
Pueblo Bonito Oceanfront Resorts and Spas
Cabo San Lucas, Baja California Sur
800.990.8250
www.pueblobonito.com

THE VISION

Create a multi-level water feature to harmonize with the minimalistic, Zen-inspired theme of the holistic sanctuary. Spanning over ninety feet with numerous elevation drops, the water feature begins on the lobby veranda. Flowing from multiple basins, water spills over a nine foot drop. A narrow spout diverts the water into a long channel, which stair-steps down the walkway. Transitions in the interior make for an intriguing contrast of textures and colors; from golden pebble, to deep blue tile and then to black Mexican river rock.

Features: Shona art sculptures
Floating candle boats
Cobalt tile

Photos Courtesy of Mary Vail, OSG Publicist

GOLD AWARDWINNER

WATER FEATURE

SILVOR
AWARDWINNER

Category: Commercial Water feature *Art
Project: Courtyard Fountain at Sunset Beach
Pueblo Bonito Oceanfront Resorts and Spas
Cabo San Lucas, Baja California Sur
49 ft

Pueblo Bonito Sunset Beach, Pueblo Bonito Oceanfront Resorts and Spas

THE VISIONARIES

Pueblo Bonito Sunset Beach
Pueblo Bonito Oceanfront Resorts and Spas

Architect/Designer: Wimberly, Allison, Tong & Goo

Collaborators: Cotur, contractor

Project Owner: Ernesto Coppel
Pueblo Bonito Oceanfront Resorts and Spas
Cabo San Lucas, Baja California Sur
800.990.8250
www.pueblobonito.com

Art Sculptures: Muvezi Gallery
www.muvezi.com

Charities: Fundacion Letty Coppel
www.lettycoppelfoundation.com
Muvezi Charitable Foundation
www.shona-african-sculptures.com

THE VISION

Create a traditional Mexican courtyard water feature with a modern architectural look. A popular gathering place, the fountain became the perfect local to create an outdoor gallery, exhibiting exquisite Shona art sculptures by Zimbabwe African artisans. Sale of the art benefits two notable charities: the Muvezi Charitable Foundation: fighting against malaria in Africa, and the Fundacion Letty Coppel: helping those most in need by advocating ecology, social work, community development, culture, and knowledge.

Features: All-tile interior
Three large pottery vessels

Photos Courtesy of Mary Vail, OSG Publicist

SILVOR AWARDWINNER

WATER FEATURE

SILVOR
AWARDWINNER

Category: Commercial Special Applications * Marine Habitat
Project: Cabo Dolphins Center
Marina Cabo San Lucas
3.5 million liters of seawater

Cabo Dolphins Center

THE VISIONARIES

Cabo Dolphins Center

Architect/Designer: Arq. Enrique Norton
Ten Arquitectos

Project Owner: Cabo Adventures
Cabo San Lucas, Mexico
888.303.2653 US toll free
01.800.365.2226 Mexico toll free
www.cabodolphins.com

THE VISION

Present a world class, safe, interactive, research and educational marine mammal encounter environment. Monitored 24 hours a day, the care and wellbeing of the dolphins are a priority. In addition to public encounters, the facility developed special programs including environmental awareness, educational encounters for students, and therapy encounters for the mentally and physically challenged. The center also operates special environmental education programs and marine mammal preservation projects. For the health of the animals, the habitat provides continuous clean, properly filtered ocean water from the Sea of Cortez.

Features: Highly controlled marine habitat
Underground viewing portals

Photos Courtesy of Mary Vail, OSG Publicist

SILVOR AWARDWINNER

SPECIAL APPLICATION

THE GAVA TEAM

Iberostar Grand Paraiso, Riviera Maya, Mexico. Photo Courtesy of Iberostar Hotel and Resorts

THE JUDGES

A panel of judges comprised of elite professionals from several disciplines reviewed and ranked the finalists. All entries were identified by a number. Entrant, builder, designer, and owner names were anonymous.

Entries were judged on their aesthetic beauty, and how each exemplified the objectives of the project: designs exhibiting original and diverse concepts demonstrating respect for environmental, cultural, philosophical, and/or historical components.

Photo Courtesy of The Art Institute of Las Vegas

Nancy K. Bohnett, IIDA
IDEC NEWH
Academic Director
The Art Institute of Las Vegas
Las Vegas, Nevada, USA
702.992.8527
nbohnett@aii.edu

Interior Designer Nancy Bohnett is head of the interior design programs at The Art Institute of Las Vegas. As academic director, she oversees departmental faculty, curriculum development, and student advising for the school's interior design, drafting technology, and design, fashion, and retail management programs.

Bohnett has a wealth of experience in the interior design industry. Her professional experience includes time spent at design and architectural firms, working on a variety of commercial and residential properties. She has worked on projects for hotel and casino clients, including Caesars Palace, MGM Grand, the Frontier, the Riviera, the Sands, and Sundance Hotel Las Vegas. The projects included guest rooms and suites, gaming and public space developments, such as Studio 54, Gatsby's, and Brown Derby, all in the MGM Grand. She also worked on the Luxor Theater, former home of the Blue Man Group.

Bohnett's skills are seen in hotel and residential properties in California, Nevada, Hawaii, Colorado, and Minnesota. She has worked from conceptual design to walk through and punch lists. Her other responsibilities included renovations, development, and coordination of master magicians Siegfried and Roy's personal properties. She was a member of Disney's Imagineering Department at Euro Disney in France. She also found success in business development, marketing and sales with International Woodwork Corporation. She instructed at Colorado State University. She served as a regional design consultant for Best Western International, assisting with design standards and updates for properties in nine states.

Bohnett is an active member of the Network of the Hospitality Industry (NEWH), International Interior Design Association (IIDA), and the American Society of Interior Designers (ASID) professional organizations. She holds her National Council for Interior Design Qualification (NCIDQ) license. She is also licensed by the Nevada State Board of Architecture and Design. She is pursuing a master's degree, earned a bachelor's degree in interior design from the University of Arizona, and an associate degree in art history from Briarcliff College.

Photo Courtesy of Charles A. Kubat

Charles A. Kubat, AIA,
AICP, LEED-AP
Founder/President
Kubat Consulting, LLC
Las Vegas, Nevada, USA
702.242.9549
kubatconsulting@cox.net

Architect and urban designer Charles A. Kubat is the founder and president of Kubat Consulting, LLC, a firm providing development management services to landowners, builders, and developers. The firm also specializes in community planning and design services as part of multi-disciplinary teams for public and private-sector projects.

In a career spanning more than 38 years, Kubat has provided personal design services and led design and planning teams around the world. This multi-disciplined architect/planner has numerous design awards to his credit. He's licensed in Nevada, Colorado, and Maryland, as well as carrying the National Council of Architectural Registration Boards (NCARB) designation. He has completed architecture and urban design/planning projects in California, Maryland, Massachusetts, Virginia, Tennessee, Texas, Florida, New Jersey, Illinois, Louisiana, Colorado, Arizona, Minnesota, and Nevada.

Kubat provides his unique multi-disciplined design perspective to a wide range of projects, including long-range planning for downtown redevelopment and planned communities, conceptual architectural design projects for retail, mixed use, office, resort, new village planning, master planning, business parks, landscape, streetscape, signage, and monument design. He creates strategies for sustainability, redevelopment, urban design, high-density housing, overall community programming, custom and production residential development.

Kubat's diverse portfolio includes design and management for residential and commercial entities, cultural and sports-themed venues such as zoos, museums, art centers, golf courses, recreation clubs with swimming pools, neighborhood parks, and major sports stadium complexes.

Kubat spent more than eight years as the vice-president of planning and design for the Howard Hughes Corp. (an affiliate of The Rouse Co.) for Summerlin in Las Vegas, one of the most successful U.S. master-planned communities, encompassing 22,500 acres, 70,000 units, and 23.6 million square feet of commercial/employment /institutional uses. Summerlin led the country in master-planned community home sales for ten straight years. With his design leadership, Summerlin received recognition as the Urban Land Institute 2002 Master Planned Community of the Year for its design, financial success, and community infrastructure.

Prior to Hughes, Kubat served as director of design and planning at Friendswood Development Co. in Houston, and as a vice president and principal of RTKL Associates Inc. in Baltimore.

As an educator, Kubat has shared his knowledge and experience lecturing at prominent institutions across the U.S. Graduating summa cum laude from the University of Minnesota, Kubat earned a Bachelor of Arts and Bachelor of Science in architecture. He earned a master's in city planning from Massachusetts Institute of Technology. He studied resort planning and design at Harvard University. He is also an accredited professional in U.S. Green Building Council's Leadership in Energy and Environmental Design (LEED) certification program.

Photo Courtesy of Melissa Menard

Melissa Menard
Principal
Pieces Fine Art
Los Angeles, California, USA
310.729.9726
www.piecesfineart.com
melissa@piecesfineart.com

From public spaces to public places, to the intimacy of a cottage in the Adirondacks, curator Melissa Menard has always believed that, regardless of the venue, art is a very personal experience.

For more than 20 years she has been connecting exceptional works by emerging and mid-career artists to discriminating corporate and private collectors. Her philosophy is that artistic expression lies not only in the eye-of-the-artist, but in the soul-of-the-collector.

Menard's fascination of art began at the young age of six when her father purchased the initial piece of the family's now major art collection. From that point, Menard accompanied him on buying trips across the country, amassing notable pieces by Salvador Dali, Marc Chagall, Whistler, Joan Miro, and Leroy Neiman.

After graduating from Western Michigan University with a Bachelors in Business, Menard joined the family business, Menard Premiere Builders in Detroit. Her responsibilities included "everything to do with a custom home development," from buying raw land, to construction design, building, and interior design. A specialist in fine art placement, she designed, built, and curated three major art galleries for the company.

Moving to California with her husband in 2000, Menard decided to concentrate on art, soon establishing herself as one of the top private curators in the city. She has established individual collections worth over $2 million.

Through public exhibitions, private "Salon Previews," and even via the internet, Menard's mission is to ensure that great works of art and collectors have an avenue and environment by which they may come together and form a relationship through a mutual experience.

On Menard's highly toured site, www.piecesfineart.com, international collectors have the opportunity to acquire exquisite pieces, as well as place objects de'art in the curators unique secondary art market catalog for sale, all in a confidential one-on-one transaction, insuring privacy for both parties.

Melissa's art career is tightly woven into her real estate business, www.justaskmelissa.com. Always searching for the ultimate in individual experiences, her passion has enabled her to meld a client's personal art appreciation with their own personal space.

Living in the heart of Los Angeles, Menard's client list includes the movers and shakers of the vibrant city, including television and film moguls, celebrities, musicians, sports figures, and politicians. On the artist side, she has represented rock 'n' roll stars turned artists such as Ronnie Wood of the Rolling Stones and Grace Slick of Jefferson Airplane.

Years of involvement with commercial and residential development, she appreciates the importance and the impact art has on an environment.

Menard has woven her passion into helping those in need; since 2002 she has devoted time and resources for the Los Angeles Make-a-Wish Foundation Annual Art & Wine Tasting Event.

The artisans at KREISS create unique luxury outdoor furnishings in which to enjoy award winning water-inspired environments.
Photo Courtesy of Mary Vail, OSG, Publicist

2009 GAVA SPONSORS

STRUCTURE STUDIOS®
3D Software Development Company

Presenting Sponsor

Structure Studios is a software development company specializing in 3-D visualization with groundbreaking products like Pool Studio/Pool Design Software, an innovative computer-based program that allows designers to transform 2-D concept to 3-D virtual tours. Pool Studio transforms an ordinary flat design into an interactive, photorealistic 3-D environment for consumers to explore from any angle. With international headquarters based in Las Vegas, Structure Studios spans the globe with thousands of pool builders, designers, and sales consultants actively using the program in fifteen countries, including the United States, Australia, Mexico, and the United Arab Emirates. www.structurestudios.com.

brand.™

Platinum Sponsor

BRAND, Ltd. is a full-service advertising agency, specializing in effective brand development, positioning, and marketing strategies. By developing distinct, results-driven methodologies, BRAND earned its reputation as a proven leader in the full-service marketing paradigm. The company's techniques are tested, but always flexible and forward-looking. It takes a holistic approach to clients' business goals and objectives that empower them to succeed. Through detailed research, led by an award-winning team, a tailor-made strategy is produced for each client through an understanding of the client's product and target market. www.brandltd.com.

ZODIAC POOL SYSTEMS, INC.

Platinum Sponsor

Zodiac Pool Systems, Inc., a subsidiary of Zodiac Marine & Pool and a Carlyle Group portfolio company, is a world leader in swimming pool and spa products. The company's comprehensive product lines are marketed under the leading brand names of Baracuda®, Jandy®, Nature2®, Polaris®, and Cover Pools®. Zodiac Pool Systems is the leading provider of premium, innovative pool and spa products. It's committed to designing and producing the most energy efficient, earth-friendly pool products and systems available. www.zodiacpoolsystems.com or www.jandy.com.

Paramount
Pool Life. Simplified.

Gold Sponsor

Paramount Pool and Spa Systems is the world's leader in floor cleaning systems, with a history of innovation since 1964. An American manufacturer with a pool building heritage, located in Chandler, Arizona, Paramount offers six premier in-floor cleaning systems. It offers Virginia Graeme Baker 2008 compliant safety drains, Clear O3 water purification systems, JetPaks for the ultimate in-ground spa therapy, water features and many other innovative products. www.1paramount.com.

THREE V ENTERPRISES

Three V Enterprises, established in Las Vegas in 2008, is devoted to developing platforms to honor, educate and inspire architects, designers, builders, manufacturers, and developers worldwide.

Photo Courtesy of Virginia Martino

VIRGINIA MARTINO

A highly respected branding and marketing professional, Martino has excelled in creating successful promotional, marketing, and branding strategies for a wealth of high-profile clientele. Her diversified clientele list includes professional organizations, gaming resorts, residential/commercial real estate, medical, financial, and retail markets. She guides her team of creative designers, marketing strategists, and writers to achieve hundreds of awards for her company and clients.

Martino is founder/president of Brand, Ltd., a diverse full-service advertising agency. Martino is also the co-founder and president of The Odyssey Lifestyle, producer of wine, food, and lifestyle events.

Martino has won more than fifty national American Corporate Identity Awards of Excellence, fifteen Addy Awards, including best of show, twelve Addy Awards of Excellence, four Pinnacle Awards of Excellence, an Award of Merit from the Public Relations Society of America, and was featured in the Big Book of Design for Business and websites. She is included in the Nationwide Register's *Who's Who in Executives and Businesses in 2000-2001 and 2002-2003*, and one of the 2002 Distinguished Women in Southern Nevada. www.brandltd.com.

JOSEPH M. VASSALLO, CBP

Photo Courtesy of Jerry Metellus, Photography

Author, designer, entrepreneur, and innovator, Joseph Vassallo's talents extend well beyond his award-winning firm, Paragon Pools of Las Vegas.

Vassallo's innovative design concepts and business acumen are celebrated in a multitude of arenas, from consumer and business publications to electronic and Web media. His eagerness to employ special materials has resulted in major trend-setting applications. Vassallo's projects were featured in many television segments, including an HGTV special. The firm's project list includes pools for major hotels, casino moguls, celebrated chefs, celebrities, luxury home tours, and multiple man-made lake renovations.

Vassallo sits on local, regional, and national boards for the Association of Pool and Spa Professionals (APSP). He has served many years on the National Builders Council and was a contributor to the association's foremost technical publication, the *APSP Builders Manual 3rd Edition*.

Vassallo's Certified Building Professional (CBP) credentials designate him as one of the pool industry's elite. He presents seminars for international symposiums. He contributes to technical manuals, mentors novice designers, and works with local, state and national legislators impacting licensing, standards, building codes, and safety regulations.

Vassallo's humanitarian works involving educational and water safety programs earned him acclaim, including Citizen of Distinction and The Jefferson Award.

Paragon Pools is the only Nevada pool builder named to the AQUA 100 best pool companies in the nation, and to the Aqua 100 Hall of Fame as named by *AQUA Magazine*. Vassallo won best pool in the 2009 Las Vegas Parade of Homes and he was named 2009 Master of Design by Pool and Spa News, and entrepreneur of the year in 2009 by the Las Vegas Chamber of Commerce Big E awards.

His design and lifestyle book, *The Al Fresco Life: Pools, Spas, Bars & Kitchens,* was released in 2008 by Schiffer Publishing. www.paragonpools.net.

MARY B. VAIL, OSG

A public relations and marketing guru, author, photographer, and publicist, Mary Vail has successfully placed clients in prestigious international publications, television broadcasts, radio spots, and websites.

She co-authored and photographed, *The Al Fresco Life: Pools, Spas, Bars and Kitchens*, a design and lifestyle book benefiting homeless education programs.

As founder and president of Mary Vail, OSG Publicist, an independent public relations firm, she specializes in image building campaigns and focuses her energies on positive publicity. The Las Vegas firm has designed and managed successful innovative marketing and promotional campaigns for an array of organizations, from aerospace to sports marketing.

Known as the philanthropic publicist, Vail seeks ways to improve the educational, physical, or socio-economic lifestyle of those less fortunate. Vail has garnered numerous awards and prestigious accolades including being knighted Lady Mary Vail, Dame of Grace in the Order of Saint George – Knights of Malta. She has received the highest individual community service award from the Public Relations Society of America, the Paul M. Lund Public Service Award. In addition to these honors, she has also received multiple Addy Awards, MarCom Creative Design Awards, W3 Web Design Awards, and numerous proclamations and congressional citations. Vail is a graduate of the University of Hawaii. www.maryvailpublicist.com

---

GAVA ADVISORY BOARD

Mark V. Martino
Master Architect

Noah Nehlich
Owner and Founder, Structure Studios

Sean Vail
Technology Consultant